Bonsai

A Wisley Handbook

Bonsai

ALAN ROGER

Cassell

The Royal Horticultural Society

THE ROYAL HORTICULTURAL SOCIETY

Cassell Educational Limited
Wellington House, 125 Strand
London WC2R 0BB
for the Royal Horticultural Society

First published 1981
New edition, fully revised and reset 1985
Second impression June 1986
Third impression, revised, July 1987
Fourth impression July 1988
Fifth impression June 1989
Third edition 1990
Second impression 1991
Third impression 1992
Reprinted with corrections 1993
Reprinted 1995

British Library Cataloguing in Publication Data
Roger, A. S.
  Bonsai.
  1. Bonsai. Cultivation
  I. Title
  635.9772

ISBN 0-304-32001-3

Line drawings by Peter Mennim
Photographs by Mrs Susan Clark, Jacqui Hurst, Alan Roger,
Bill Jordan, Harry Smith Horticultural Photographic
Collection and Michael Warren

Special thanks are due to Peter Chan who lent many of his
trees for photography.

Typeset by Chapterhouse Ltd., Formby
Printed in Hong Kong by Wing King Tong Co. Ltd

Cover: common larch, *Larix decidua*, grown in root over rock style.
Photograph by Jacqui Hurst
p. 1: a Japanese maple in formal upright style.
Photograph by Wilf Halliday
p. 2: a group planting of spruce in a shallow dish.
Back cover: a group of white spruce, *Picea glauca* var. *albertiana* 'Conica'.
Photograph by Michael Warren

Contents

Introduction

The art of bonsai has been practised for many centuries in Japan, and even longer in China. The characters and meaning are the same in both languages: 'a plant in a container'. The Chinese also use the word Penjing, particularly for a miniature landscape. Although Europeans must have seen specimens in both countries from the sixteenth and seventeenth centuries onwards, the first real impact on western appreciation only came early this century with a Paris exhibition in about 1898, followed by one in London in 1909.

In China there are roughly two schools of taste – northern and southern. The latter tends towards the 'baroque' with lavish use of rock-work. The Chinese love of an object that suggests the form of an animal or bird, for example, often influences them in the choice and development of material. An extreme case exists where a bonsai is trained to look like a plant rising from a vase. There is, too, a tendency at times to topiarise the branches of ever-

Opposite: above, a mountain maple, *Acer palmatum*, in informal upright style; below, *Cryptomeria japonica* in formal upright style
Below: an early nineteenth century gouache showing bonsai displayed before a Chinese temple

greens into slightly formal planes. There are of course many classic examples of naturalism as well.

People are inevitably influenced by what they see around them in parks and gardens, as well as in the wild, a factor which has led occasionally to the unconscious development in Britain of a native style of bonsai. Oriental influences, nevertheless, are paramount among most bonsai cultivators.

More Japanese than Chinese literature on the subject has been available to the west, which has meant that western practitioners and amateurs have usually turned to the Japanese school for inspiration. Japanese influence is paramount also in the USA, especially on the west coast where Americans of Japanese origin have done so much to spread the interest in bonsai.

The principles of cultivation in both China and Japan are the same. It is in the end result that one finds differences.

Penjing, from a private collection in England, making use of water and creating a pair of islands

The cultivation of bonsai is an art in the truest sense, as it entails the subordination and handling of material, albeit living, to an aesthetic end. The difference between it and other plastic arts, such as sculpture and painting, is that in the latter cases a completed work is finite, only later requiring the attention of the conservationist – whereas a bonsai, however fine, needs control and training throughout its life.

Many people are fascinated by the age of a bonsai, and pay scant attention to its aesthetic quality. The important thing, however, is the beauty or lack of it in the object before one's eyes. The age of a bonsai is only a secondary consideration. The bonsai, that is the plant and its container, must make a satisfying unity.

The late Ian Melville Clark defined a bonsai as a tree grown in a container, conforming in all respects to a normal tree except for its miniature size. It is this aspect of Bonsai which interests

A fuchsia in informal upright style

An ornamental crab apple, *Matus baccata mandshurica*, grown in informal upright style

western cultivators, and with which this booklet is most concerned; but, bearing in mind the real meaning of the word, the Japanese and Chinese also cultivate grasses, including bamboo, shrubs and other plants such as chrysanthemums in bonsai conditions. The last, in particular, are grown in all the styles in which the dwarfed trees are classified. However interesting these sorts of bonsai may be, they cannot have the long life of a tree and therefore are of less enduring value.

In theory, any tree may be made into a bonsai, but some have characteristics which make them unsuitable or uncontrollable.

10

Chamaecyparis obtusa in octopus style, at least 200 years old

Examples are those which have brittle shoots, and are therefore difficult to train; naturally contorted forms such as *Robinia pseudoacacia* 'Tortuosa' or *Salix matsudana* 'Tortuosa' or any other tree which has too much will of its own; trees with extra large leaves, fruits or flowers. Steps can be taken to reduce the size of leaves, at any rate to a limited extent, but fruits and flowers will always remain normal. It can be seen, therefore, that outsize apples, for example, on a tree a foot or even two feet high must look ridiculous.

11

The aim is to produce, in miniature, a tree that gives the illusion, when set by itself against a plain background, of a mature specimen. Plants which branch well and have small leaves, flowers or fruits are necessarily the best subjects.

Hardy trees used as bonsai must normally be kept out of doors and, subject to the restriction of their containers, in as near natural conditions as possible. They should only be brought into a room with its dry atmosphere and inadequate light for occasional display. Too long indoors can cause damage to a tree and even death. Such damage may not always be immediately apparent. In the case of evergreens, the first danger signs are the increased rate of browning of needles on conifers and leaf fall on broadleaf evergreens. In the case of deciduous trees, the shrivelling of leaves during the growing season is the first warning.

Tender bonsai are usually kept in heated or unheated greenhouses. They, too, should not be kept long in a room away from the normal light and humidity of atmosphere to which they are accustomed.

Many people have thought that there is a special mystery in the making of a bonsai; but the technique of growing plants continually in the same container has in fact long been practised in Europe. Before the First World War large gardens with ample staff and glasshouses produced grape vines, orange trees, peach trees and so on in pots which were put on display not only in the garden but on grand occasions in the house. Such plants were pruned and root pruned annually and re-potted in their original containers. It is only in the end product that the difference lies between what European gardeners aimed at and what a bonsai cultivator wants to achieve.

A fine specimen of *Juniperus rigida*, over 100 years old

Opposite: above, *Pinus parviflora*, the Japanese white pine, imported
from Japan and more than 85 years old (note the placing in the pot
slightly to the left, with the balance of the trunk to the right); below,
Ulmus procera, the English elm, grown in Chinese root over rock style
and about 20 years old
Above: ivy on a rock, grown from a cutting taken 20 years ago

Sources of material

There are now several good commercial sources of bonsai. Florist shops frequently offer plants, but they are rarely of the highest quality, and, as the retailers are unlikely to have been the original growers, they may not be able to say how long the plant has been potted and how well established it is as a bonsai. There is also the risk that the plant has been indoors too long before sale and therefore liable to delayed damage. It is re-emphasised that hardy trees should always be kept out-of-doors, except for very short periods of display.

Good bonsai nurseries, which are not only importers of fine examples from Japan but also skilled growers of indigenous material, offer trees at a wide range of prices, but beginners are advised not to aim too high and be tempted by a really important specimen until some knowledge of methods of cultivation and training have been acquired. A really finely developed bonsai is a great responsibility, being a mature work of art with many years of work and care behind it.

Common trees suitable for beginners, easily found in Britain, include: ash, beech, birch, cotoneaster, hawthorn, hornbeam, horse chestnut, ivy, juniper, larch, certain maples, oak, rowan.

The foregoing may easily be acquired in variety. Some maples are not always easy for beginners but *Acer campestre* is a native and easily manageable.

Fuchsias make good flowering subjects but must be trained to look tree like. Small flowered types are best. There are recorded specimens in this country of over 100 years old, grown in containers.

COLLECTING FROM THE WILD

Apart from buying a good tree developed by someone else, the best source by far is from collection of mature material in the wild. Such places as old quarries, cliffs, hill-tops, banks where self-sown trees have been stunted by poor conditions, strong winds or grazing animals often provide specimens of a certain

Opposite: a group planting of hornbeam, *Carpinus*, trained in Britain

age with good and picturesque trunks which may be extracted with care. A good naturally tapered trunk is thus procured while the head may be thereafter trained to the collector's taste. Old hedging which is being grubbed up can also provide good basic material and derelict gardens may also be a worthwhile source. See also Appendix III for the code of practice for collecting in the wild.

Juniperus chinensis in slanting style, over 80 years old

A good area for tree hunting

The best time to lift a tree is in the early spring as the buds are beginning to swell. This condition will depend on local climate, altitude and latitude of the specimen.

A tree may be too large or too well established to lift at once. Deciding whether a tree should be dealt with in stages depends on the estimate of the size of its root system. Preliminary excavation of the soil will reveal how far the main roots run before branching. They may reach inaccessibly into cracks in a rock, or, as can happen in the case of junipers, run for many feet underground before branching. It is wise in such cases to induce a fine root system as close as possible to the bole before lifting. To achieve this cut a circle as deep as possible round the tree, 1 to 3 feet in diameter (30–90 cm) according to its size. Excavate carefully the earth inside the circle to a width of 3 to 6 inches (8–15 cm) and trim off any ragged ended roots with sharp cutters or a knife and then in-fill with damp loam, leafmould and sharp sand; peat may be used mixed with loam and sharp sand if leafmould is unavailable. The tree should then be left undisturbed for one or two years until new feeder roots have formed in the encircling compost. If any periods of drought occur during this operation, ensure that the compost does not dry out.

The head of the tree should be lightly pruned straight away, bearing in mind one's plan for the ultimate shape.

When the moment comes to lift the tree, dig out the outer rim of the trench, sever any vertical roots which still anchor the tree, take as much as possible of the earth clinging to the new roots and wrap the whole plant in polythene to prevent drying out, if any appreciable distance home has to be covered. The tree, on reaching home, should only be put into a bonsai pot if no major roots have to be cut. Otherwise plant it in a large temporary container, such as tub, or in a cool and shady part of the garden. The latter course has the advantage that less watering may be necessary. In a container, good drainage is essential and regular spraying overhead is advisable until the tree is obviously healthily established. The soil in the pot or the ground must never be allowed to dry out. Only when the tree is well settled, possibly one or two years later, should it be placed in its final container.

Saplings and other small trees, when growing in reasonably good soil and with none of the difficult conditions dealt with above, may certainly be lifted with use of a spade or trowel in the usual way in the dormant season.

It may be that the only opportunity of procuring a tree otherwise easy to lift, for example, when on holiday, is not during its dormant period. In this case, there is a fair chance of success if as much of the soil round the tree as possible can be lifted with it to

cause the least disturbance to the root. The whole root-ball should
be wrapped in damp moss, or if none is available, damp paper.
Larger branches should be shortened and the whole tree sprayed
with water and wrapped in polythene sheeting to prevent drying
out on the way home. Once there, the tree is best plunged into a
shady part of the garden and regularly watered and sprayed overhead until signs of recovery are evident. If no garden is available
the tree should be placed in a large temporary container and
treated in the same way.

Juniperus rigida, with the trunk trained to give the effect of storm
damage to an ancient tree

OTHER SOURCES

Subjects for bonsai cultivation may be obtained from all sources of plant material – seeds, cuttings, graftings, layers, self-sown seedlings and even nursery grown trees if some unusual species is required. The last, however, is not always a very fruitful field as the trees on offer may' be standards or half standards.

A note of warning about raising bonsai from seed. Some people imagine that trees raised from seed, especially of Japanese maples, will grow into fine bonsai without assistance. This is by no means so. To raise a tree from seed merely means that it is under one's control from the start of its life. As soon as it begins to make more than one pair of leaves then its training may begin. That is, such preliminaries as setting the seedling at an angle in its pot to induce a natural seeming bend in the later development of the trunk may then be done. The pinching out of the leading shoot may be left until the height has been reached at which the trunk is required before branching is developed. Any other curves desired in the young tree may be done by wiring or tying, as described under training (see pp. 29–45).

All early development from seed is best carried out in temporary containers, with the ultimate plan in one's mind.

Below: a berberis seedling collected in a private garden, root over rock style

Above: *Juniperus chinensis* cascade style in antique
Chinese pot, on a Chinese blackwood stand; below, *Acer palmatum*,
twin trunked, imported from Japan and over 60 years old

Styles

The Japanese recognise at least 29 different styles of bonsai, but the basic ones for single trunked trees are formal upright, informal upright, slanting, semi cascade and cascade.

These main forms can appear in most of the other variants of style such as 'root over rock', 'drift-wood', 'wind-swept', 'octopus' and any of the multiple trunked groups whether grown from a common root or as separate trees. Indeed, whatever one does in forming a bonsai, it is almost bound to fall into some category, even if one has begun the training without any preconception of a style.

Examples of six basic styles:
Above, left: formal upright. Above, right: informal upright.
Opposite: Top left: semi cascade; top right: cascade.
Below left: windswept; *below right:* slanting.

There is no maximum height for bonsai, but a desirable height is relative to the size of the container. There is, however, a category known by the Japanese word – *mame*. In this case, the tree and container together must be no higher than 6 inches (15 cm).

There is a misconception in the minds of some people that small bonsai are potted on to become larger specimens as time passes. This is not so, as a general rule. Having decided on the overall size the owner wishes, the tree will live in its same container for the rest of its life, and only occasionally circumstances may make it right or necessary to change direction.

Zelkova serrata in formal upright style, with the leaves turning in autumn

Above: larch in slanting style, well blended and set with rocks
Below: European larch, *Larix decidua*, in a combination of styles –
driftwood, slanting, windswept; collected in Scotland and about 40
years old

Above: Scots pine, *Pinus sylvestris*, with twin trunk
Below: *Acer buergerianum* in root over rock style

Training

Training of a future bonsai can hardly begin too soon, and control must continue throughout its life. The aim is not only to induce a look of maturity as soon as possible, but also to prevent it losing its shape in later years. There are a number of methods usable – (a) pruning, (b) wiring, (c) tying, (d) bracing, (e) wedging, (f) weighting, (g) leaf stripping, (h) trunk thickening.

(a) Pruning includes the removal of large unwanted branches, pinching back new growth while it is still soft, and trimming newly mature growth of the past year during the winter or early spring.

If a large branch is removed, it should be taken as close to its base as possible and the remaining bark round the wound trimmed with a sharp knife. This will induce callusing and add to the aged look of the tree.

Soft, current year's growth, unless it is intended to grow in a new branch, may be pinched out with finger and thumb, or cut with scissors. New shoots are likely to appear throughout the spring and summer, especially if the tree is healthy or has recently been repotted. These should normally be shortened to two leaves. This should be done whenever an unwanted shoot develops, throughout the season.

When pruning new hard wood in winter or spring, cut cleanly up to the bud pointing in the direction in which the next shoot is required to grow.

(b) To make the best use of wiring requires a certain amount of practice. Wires of different thicknesses are required, especially if the subject under training is raw material to be shaped from scratch. The best time to tackle deciduous trees is immediately after the leaves are fully developed in spring and while branches are still reasonably pliable. Evergreens can be dealt with in autumn and winter.

Plastic coated wire is safest as it tends to mark the bark of trees less than uncoated wire. If a trunk is to be wired, insert the end of the wire well into the ground close to the bole. Then wind it spirally up the trunk and on up any branch whose position or direction of growth is to be altered. Careful bending should be done as the wiring proceeds. For smaller branches, wires may be anchored round the trunk at the base of the branch. Great care must be taken with brittle-branched plants like rhododendrons, azaleas, and laburnums. These last also have the complication of a skin-like bark which is loose on young growth, and a branch may die off if too tightly bound, or left wired too long.

It is most important to remove wires after 3 to 6 months from deciduous trees, and after 1 year from conifers such as pines, or the bark will become scarred with spiral marks.

Wiring of a bonsai tree

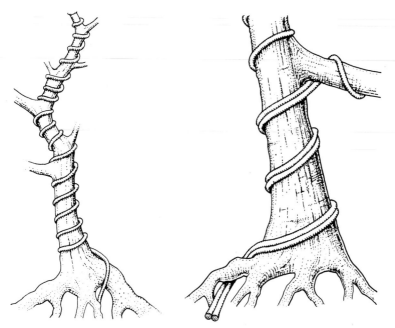

Above: application of wires to trunk and branches.
Below: Japanese white pine, *Pinus parviflora*, showing wiring of the branches

(c) Garden string can also be used to change direction of branches in cases where there is no need to alter their basic shape. It is especially practical for drawing branches in a downward direction, by passing it over the branch and under the container, or fixing to a small stake driven into the soil in the pot. A small pad should be placed between the branch and string to avoid damaging the bark. In such cases the string can usually be left on until it rots. (N.B. Untarred string should be used.)

(d) Bracing is rarely used and only to deal with heavy, but misshapen trunks (see below).

(e) Wedging can be used to part closely crossing trunks or heavy branches (see opposite), though care must be taken to avoid splitting off one side of the fork from the trunk below, through overstrain.

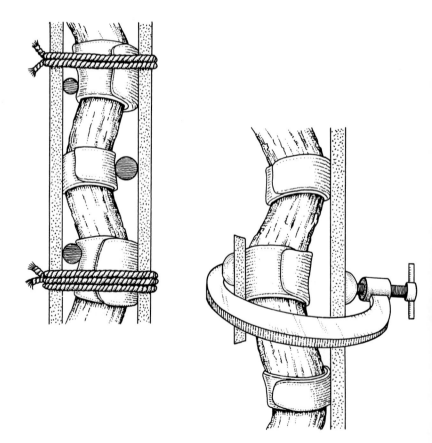

Bracing a misshapen trunk, a form of training rarely necessary.

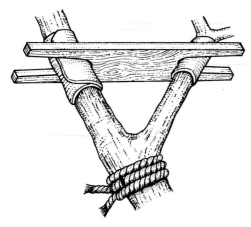

Wedges may be used to part closely crossing branches. Wooden wedges are usually used, but the bark needs to be protected from pressure

(f) Weights suspended by twine may be used to lower the angle of a branch (page 34). As in the case of (c) above, the use of a pad between twine and branch is advisable.

(g) Deciduous trees may have their leaves stripped in early summer to induce a second crop which will be smaller. When defoliating, it is best to cut the leaf at its base, leaving the petiole to fall of its own accord when the new bud at its base develops. This should not be done to evergreens, with the possible exception of ivy. A secondary benefit is the extra branchlet development which results. After this operation, the bonsai should be placed in full sun to encourage the new growth. Overhead spraying in the evening also helps.

Above: weights and ties may be used to alter the position of certain branches (see p. 33).

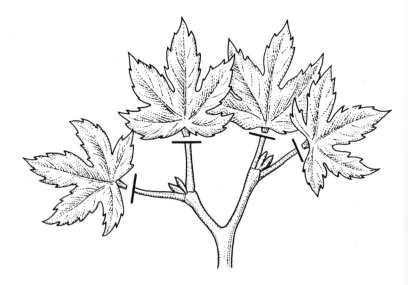

Deciduous trees may have their leaves stripped in early summer to obtain a second crop of smaller leaves.

(h) Trunks of trees will increase their girth more rapidly in the ground than when potted. It may be beneficial, therefore, occasionally to remove a slow developing bonsai from its pot and return it to the open ground for one or more years. If this is done, training of the head must continue in the usual way. The tree should be lifted annually in early spring and any vigorous roots shortened as though the tree was to be re-potted.

POTTING AND RE-POTTING

During the period of early training of raw material, any container will do provided there is good drainage and appropriate soil therein. During this early stage the shortening of the tap root and inducement of surface roots must take place, with regular re-potting until the tree is judged ready for its final home. As in the case of mature bonsai, operations affecting the root system should be carried out in early spring. It should then be placed in a good suitable container, in which it will be expected to pass the rest of its life.

A bonsai stand at one of the RHS shows

Ceramic pots should be high fired (i.e. stoneware or porcelain), to withstand frost damage in winter; there must be good drainage holes, no glaze internally and preferably with monochrome glazes externally. The Chinese and Japanese unglazed (Yi-shing type) pots are also suitable. Pots which have an incurved top are liable to frost damage due to the swelling of the soil when a thaw sets in.

If plantings are made on flat pieces of stone, holes should be drilled through them, not for drainage, but for fixing ties to secure the trees to a flat surface. Containers have also been successfully made from concrete treated to look like weathered stone. The rubbing of farmyard manure on the surface of concrete will encourage the growth of algae and a weathered appearance.

A group of swamp cypress, *Taxodium distichum*, an unusual bonsai subject

It is most important when potting a tree in its permanent home to select a container which will harmonise with it, for a tree and its container must make an aesthetically satisfactory whole. As a rule the base of the trunk should be placed off-centre, except, perhaps, in the case of the formal upright style. Imagine the tree and its container to be set inside a rectangular frame, and it will easily be seen whether or not it has a good balance in the way that an artist composes a picture. The tree should be mounded slightly so that when it is seen at eye-level, the bole is visible above the rim of its container. The soil should slope down to slightly below the rim so that water may be caught there. Before inserting the tree, all damaged roots should be sharply trimmed.

Acer palmatum 'Seigen', remarkable for its foliage

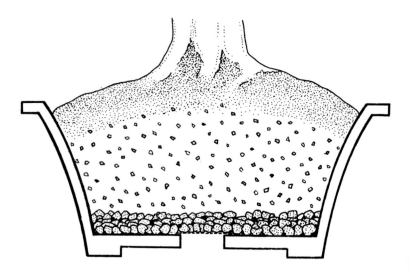

Diagram to show the correct placing of a tree in a pot and gradation of soil. The bole of the tree is raised above the rim, with room at the rim for water to settle.

The soil should consist usually of equal parts of loam, leafmould and sharp sand. Peat may be used, if leafmould is unavailable, but it is largely only a moisture retainer with little nutritional value. Proportions may be altered according to the consistency of the loam or the type of tree to be planted. For instance pines prefer a sandier mixture. Slow acting fertilizers, such as bone meal, Osmocote, and basic slag, may be mixed in, in moderation. The compost should then be sifted into three grades, coarsely granulated, medium and fine.

The drainage holes are best covered with perforated zinc or plastic gauze; crocks may be used but take up precious space in shallow containers. The coarse granules are placed to cover the bottom of the container and the tree held in the desired position. The medium soil is then introduced and worked in round all the roots. A blunt stick or fingers may be used to make sure all spaces are filled. The finest soil is then used as top dressing.

If a tree seems likely to be top heavy in its pot then wires or strong twine should be passed over the root system and secured under the pot, having been passed through the drainage holes. If there is only one hole a piece of wood may be placed across the drainage hole, on the underside, round which the ties may be secured. The ties can usually be removed later when the tree has made enough new root to secure itself.

Wire used to secure a tree in a pot with two drainage holes, using wire or strong string.

Securing a tree in a pot when there is only one drainage hole: the tie is secured round a piece of wood.

The newly potted bonsai should then be carefully watered until it is certain that the soil is well saturated. It should then be kept in a shady position outside for a month, when new root growth should have begun. Do not overwater in that period, but equally ensure that there is no drying out of the soil. There will probably be no need to re-pot for two or three years, except in the case of trees with a vigorous root action such as larches and birches which may need annual attention. Willows which can readily be grown from cuttings are known, in many varieties, for their extreme vigour of growth. For example, if a bonsai of *Salix babylonica* or *S. × chrysocoma*, both weeping forms, is attempted, the root development is such that root-pruning and re-potting twice a year is necessary – in early spring and again in summer.

A weeping willow in an antique Chinese pot on a Chinese blackwood stand; vigorous spring growth will be severly pruned when the plant is repotted in August

The twisted trunk is a beautiful feature of the pomegranate, *Punica granatum*, although fruit and flowers, if allowed to develop, would probably look out of proportion on this fine specimen; Japanese trained

In each case one half of the roots are removed. In the spring operation only light tidying of the branches may be necessary, but in summer all previous season's whippy growth should be taken back to one or two buds. The ensuing new growth provides the delicate look required in late spring when the new leaves unfold. Willows require plenty of water. Indeed after the summer re-potting it is as well to stand the pot in a container of water.

The foregoing advice applies when the framework of the tree is developed, and not in the early stages while the basic trunk and branches are being created.

In the case of pines the soil requirements are different and a mixture of two parts sharp sand and one each of loam and leaf-mould is best. Re-potting need not take place for from three to five years, as with most evergreens. The roots of Scots pines (*Pinus sylvestris*) offer a slight problem as they are liable to bleed when damaged. If it is a large root, a tourniquet will help, but cauterisation, after sharply cutting off the damaged root, is effective.

Juniperus rigida, approximately 160 years old

ROOT PRUNING

It is at the re-potting stage that root pruning takes place, and the best time for this is early spring for deciduous trees. Evergreens may be re-potted even as late as the end of March or early April, provided, in the case of pines, that the new shoots have not begun to develop too much. The tree is lifted from the pot and old soil shaken out, and a blunt stick is used to tease out impacted soil from among the central root ball. All roots should be gently spread out like hair before severing about one third of their length with a sharp knife or cutters. Surface roots may also be trimmed leaving only important ones which radiate from the bole and whose visibility helps the appearance of age. Trimming of the head of the tree should also take place simultaneously, to some extent to balance the loss of root but also to maintain the basic shape. When the branches are bare it offers the best chance to study the branch system. Current young growth will already have been dealt with during the tree's active period, but, especially in the case of vigorous trees such as larch, birch and beech, it is possible to judge from the development of the buds how far it is desirable to prune back mature branchlets. The tree is then returned to its container and new soil supplied as described above.

TRAINING OVER OR ON A ROCK

Two important styles of cultivating bonsai are 'root over rock' and on a flat, irregular raft of stone. In the first case it is best to

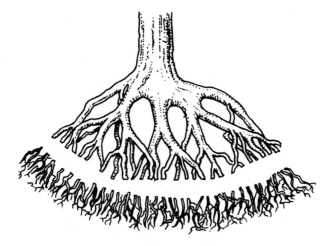

Root pruning, showing how far to cut back the roots.

start with an immature tree with fairly long roots, so that it can be placed at the top of a rock or in a crevice with its roots placed as close as possible in the crannies below. Soil should be worked in where possible and the plant secured in place with twine. A covering of sphagnum moss should be packed on top of the roots and tied over the whole, leaving the trunk and head exposed. The stone should then be placed in a pot two-thirds full of soil with the tips of the roots below the stone. The pot should then be filled to just below the rim as in normal potting. To ensure adherence of the roots to the stone the tree should be left for at least a year before exposing the 'root over the rock'. Re-potting, in due course, of such plantings takes place as usual except that the tree is never removed from the rock itself.

In the second case, the flat stone must have two or more holes drilled through which wires may be passed to secure the tree in the desired position. A small mound of potting mixture should be placed under the base of the trunk. The roots are then spread out and covered with soil which is pressed into place. The whole

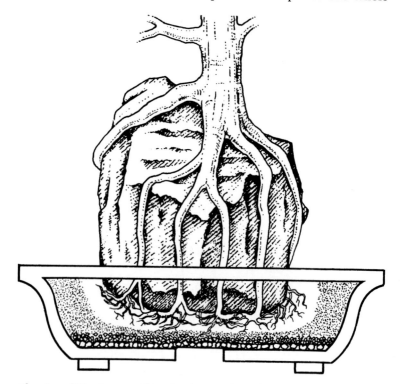

Planting of 'Root over rock' style, showing how the rock and roots are placed in the pot.

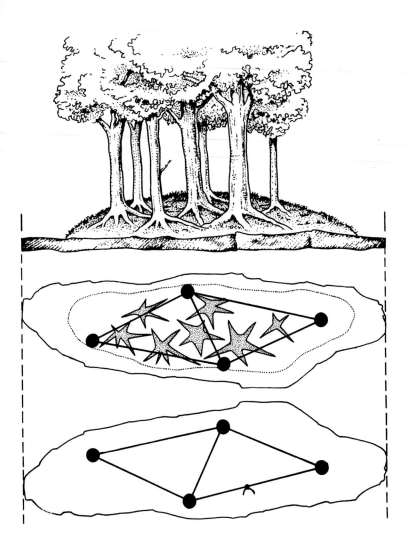

Method of securing group planting on flat stone. View of upper side before replacing soil. Below: Underside view, showing drainage holes through which anchoring wires are secured.

surface is then covered in short green moss tied into place with bass or twine, and left there until the whole arrangement has set. There being no sides to such a container and it being important not to disturb the soil and moss, great attention must be paid to subsequent watering, using a can with a fine spray or a sprayer.

Seasonal care

WATERING

If possible, use of chlorinated water directly from the tap should be avoided. But if there is no alternative, it should be left to stand for one or two days before use. Any watering can used must have a fine spray, so that the soil is dampened, but not disturbed. Enough water should be given so that it drips through the drainage holes. Sometimes waterlogging can occur due to the activity of worms impacting the soil. If possible these should be removed. A sharp but not too violent tap of the pot on a wooden surface or on a lawn will bring them to the surface to be pulled out.

The waterer must use his judgement according to the weather, depth or size of pot. For example, large leaved or deciduous trees usually need more than pines. If the weather is very hot it may be necessary to water two or three times daily. Dense headed trees, such as junipers, can prevent the rain from reaching the surface of the soil, so that wet weather can lull one into a false sense of security. Regular checking of such specimens is therefore essential.

Below: *Sargeretia theezans*, the bird plum, in split trunk style, growing in an antique Chinese stoneware pot
Opposite: above, horse chestnut, *Aesculus hippocastanum* about 30 years old; below, *Pyracantha angustifolia* with autumn berries

WEEDING AND FEEDING

Pots should be kept weeded and dead leaves and needles removed from the surface.

Apart from any fertilizer incorporated in the soil, bonsai should be fed once a week in the spring and early summer and again two or three times in the autumn before leaf fall. Best of all is water in which well rotted manure has been soaked, or dried blood sprinkled on the surface and watered in. Otherwise liquid fertilizers such as are used on roses or house plants will do. The best of these is a product like Osmocote which releases fertilizer gradually over a period of months.

PESTS

All natural pests found in a garden can attack bonsai, and the same remedies may be applied as to plants in the ground. The tree, being smaller than its bigger relatives in the ground, can be weakened or spoilt in appearance more easily, so counter action should not be neglected. Pines and larches are prone to attack by woolly aphids which are not only unsightly but dangerous to their health. Daily inspection while watering and the removal of any pests found will also help to keep matters under control.

There is a beneficial fungus to be found on the roots of some pines which can be confused at first sight with woolly aphis, but the squeezing of a piece between finger and thumb will soon reassure one. If it is an aphis the blood will mark the fingers.

PLACING AND WINTER CARE

Hardy bonsai should have as much light and air as possible: they should be indoors only for occasional display.

If there is danger from high wind they can be tied to the staging by crossed wires or twine over the pot, or stood on the ground temporarily.

Prolonged frost can cause evergreens to die of drought. In such conditions it is best to plunge the pots in straw, leaves or ashes so that the soil can be kept open and moist. Plunging one's hands through this cover to feel the soil is the best way to test the condition of the soil in the pots. Heavy snow should be brushed from branches or its weight, especially when frozen, may break or split branches.

Opposite: Cotoneasters are easy subjects for bonsai; this one is trained in informal upright style

Staging designed to protect bonsai from extreme winter weather in northern Scotland

Pots

Newcomers to the art of bonsai may have difficulty in acquiring suitable pots. Certain nurserymen and shops have imported Chinese or Japanese pots on sale at varying prices. Some amateurs make their own most successfully. Art schools and practising ·British potters are usually glad to make something different from mugs, cups and saucers, though occasionally the essential requirements of a bonsai pot have to be explained, before a satisfactory product is evolved.

Certain of the bonsai societies too have pots available for their members to buy at reasonable prices.

Chamaecyparis obtusa 'Aurea' grown octopus style in a Chinese pot and imported from Shanghai in the 1920s

Above: a maidenhair tree, *Ginkgo biloba*, approximately 100 years old
Opposite: above, a group planting over rock of Hinoki cypress,
Chamaecyparis obtusa, giving the effect of a clump in rock strewn
forest; below, a commercial display of bonsai at an RHS show

Tools

Tools should be as sharp as possible, and include a knife, secateurs, tweezers, and chisels; especially useful is a good pair of dog's nail clippers. These have a curved cutting edge which is well adapted for severing young shoots or semi-mature growth extending from rounded branches.

A turn-table when potting, three grades of sieve for soil preparation, and a small, soft brush for dealing with the soil surface are useful. The last is also handy when cleaning a surface of detritus before showing a plant.

Larix decidua, European larch, growing in root over rock style

Above: *Juniperus chinensis*, semi cascade style
Below: a group of hawthorn, *Crataegus*, showing autumn colour

Trident maple, *Acer buergerianum*, root over rock style; Japanese
trained, about 60 years old, in an unglazed Japanese pot

Appendix I Good and bad points

The following points may be of help to those judging bonsai, as well as to owners wishing to exhibit at shows.

The following are merits:

1. A strong, well shaped trunk, tapering upwards, springing naturally from the soil.
2. A good fanning out of surface roots from the base of the trunk, gradually disappearing into the soil.
3. A good, well proportioned head of branches which are well spaced and set naturally on the trunk.
4. The tree as natural looking as possible in its surroundings.
5. The pot itself, preferably in monochrome glazes, must be in proportion to the tree, to form an artistic unity. Decorated polychrome pots can, of course, be used, but may look too fussy when containing flowering or fruiting trees.
6. The tree should be placed in the pot so as to create a visual balance. For example, if the base of the trunk is towards the right-hand edge, the main weight of the head should incline leftwards.
7. Flowers or fruit, on varieties which are grown to produce these, must be as near as possible in proportion. For example, a full sized apple would look absurd on a tree one or two feet high.
8. If large leaved trees are used, fewer branches are best, so that the general effect is of an 'impressionist' order, with each leaf giving a broad sweep of green. Pinnate leaves, of course, give an illusion of a branch bearing small leaves.
9. A tree growing with its roots clasping a rock must really adhere and not merely be wrapped loosely round the rock.
10. A tree should be planted well raised up in its pot, so that the bole can be clearly seen, if viewed at eye-level, over the rim of the pot.
11. Stones and moss or other covering of the surface of the soil must look natural and well established.
12. If deciduous trees are shown in winter, scars and marks of training must be invisible.

The following are defects which should be avoided or rectified.

a. A weak, badly shaped trunk, or one which looks as though it were merely a branch stuck in the soil.

b. Badly spaced or crossed branches, or those rubbing one on another.
c. Badly cut branches that have not callused over.
d. Elaborately artificial effects, often caused by wiring into unnatural curves.
e. Snagged and abruptly cut roots visible above the soil, or dead fibrous roots standing up in the air.
f. A tree placed exaggeratedly out of balance.
g. Flowers or fruit out of proportion to the size of the tree.
h. A pot which is out of harmony with its tree. For example, a decorated polychrome pot used for flowering or fruiting species. Plastic pots are aesthetically bad.
i. Foliage which totally hides the trunk, giving the appearance of a bush instead of a tree.
j. A tree planted with the soil and bole sunk far below the rim of its container.
k. Untidy surface of the soil, and fussy, unnecessary decoration such as ill shaped, unnatural looking stones and ornaments.
l. A tree grown in a style totally alien to its species.

Below: an example of Penjing created in Britain
Opposite: above, *Pinus thunbergii* in raft style, grown from one plant to look like a group of three separate trees; below, a group of *Zelkova serrata*

Appendix II Some recommended bonsai books

Among the best books in the English language are:—

The Japanese Art of Miniature Trees and Landscapes. Their Creation, Care and Enjoyment. By Yuji Yoshimura and Giovanna M. Halford. (Published by Tuttle, Rutland, Vermont, U.S.A., 1957, 1959.)

The Art of Bonsai. By Peter Adams. Published by Ward Lock, 1981.

Successful Bonsai Growing. By Peter Adams. Published by Ward Lock, 1978.

Bonsai: its Art, Science, History and Philosophy. By Deborah R. Koreshoff. Published by Croom Helm, 1984.

Bonsai Design, Book I. By Peter Adams. Published by Peter Adams, 1985. First of a series dealing with individual species.

Bonsai: the Art of Growing and Keeping Miniature Trees. By Peter Chan. Published by Apple Press, 1986.

Other good books by Japanese authors:—

The Masters' Book of Bonsai. Compiled by the Directors of the Japan Bonsai Association. Published by Collingridge.

Practical Bonsai for Beginners. By Kenji Murata. Published by Japan Publications Trading Company.

The Mini-Bonsai Hobby. By Tel'ichi Katayama. Published by Japan Publications.

Juniperus chinensis, driftwood and informal upright style

Above: a group of *Chamaecyparis pisifera* representing a grove, with mosses and lichens as ground cover
Below: a flowering crab apple in informal upright style

Appendix III Code of practice

1. Have careful regard for the environment when contemplating collecting bonsai material.
2. Obtain permission from the landowner or agent.
3. Only consider material which is not a cash crop.
4. Only collect material according to sound horticultural practice (i.e. the material has best possible chance of survival).
5. Only collect material and quantities you can reasonably expect to survive given the appropriate aftercare.
6. Only collect if you can provide this aftercare.
7. Above all obey the countryside code and behave reasonably.

Suggested suitable sites for collecting:
Any site due for clearance for whatever reason

Inhospitable sites such as bogs or rock outcrops, where the survival of the plant would be limited

Any site where the growth of self-seeded material would probably cause a hazard, such as forestry firebreaks, ditches, sides of paths etc.

Index

Page numbers in **bold** refer to illustrations